Julian Baggini is the founding editor of *The Philosophers' Magazine*. He has a PhD on the philosophy of personal identity and is the author, co-author or editor of over twenty books including *The Pig That Wants to be Eaten*, *The Ego Trick*, *Welcome to Everytown*, *The Virtues of the Table*, and *The Edge of Reason*. He has written for numerous newspapers and magazines, as well as for the think-tanks The Institute of Public Policy Research, Demos and Counterpoint. His website is www.microphilosophy.net

ALSO BY JULIAN BAGGINI

A SHORT HISTORY

of TRUTH

Consolations for a
Post-Truth World

Julian Baggini

Quercus

First published in Great Britain in 2017 by Quercus.
This paperback edition published in 2018 by

Quercus Editions Ltd
Carmelite House
50 Victoria Embankment
London EC4Y 0DZ

An Hachette UK company

A CIP catalogue record for this book is available
from the British Library.

MMP ISBN 978 1 78648 889 3
Ebook ISBN 978 1 78648 890 9

10 9 8 7 6 5 4

Typeset by Jouve (UK), Milton Keynes

Printed and bound in the UK by Clays Ltd, Elcograf S.p.A.

'While we falsely admire and extol the powers of the human mind we neglect to seek for its true helps.'

—*Francis Bacon*[1]

Contents

CONTENTS

Introduction

When I was growing up, I discovered *The Plain Truth*. It was something of a novelty, the only free magazine stacked in pavement dump bins in my small home town. The title was worthy of a marketing award, with an extra commendation for its strapline: 'A Magazine of Understanding'. Who wouldn't want to know the truth, to understand the world? I picked one up and in time sent off for a free subscription. I wasn't alone. At its peak in 1986 the monthly had a circulation of 8.2 million copies, 2.3 million more than *Time*.

The promise of 'The Truth' has always been alluring. The most quoted gospel verse on evangelical posters and literature is John 14:6, in which Jesus proclaims, 'I am the way, the truth and the life.' It resonates because we all have a sense that truth is not merely an abstract property of propositions but somehow essential to living well. If your life turns out to have been built on nothing but lies, it is as though it has not been real. Whether you believe Jesus shows the way or not, John's promise that 'The truth shall make you free' (8:32) rings true.

Looking back now at *The Plain Truth*, however, I find the adjective in the title at least as interesting as the noun, with its supremely definite article. 'Plain' and 'simple' are among the most common descriptors of truth, because that is often exactly how the truth seems. Paris is the capital of France, George Washington was the first President of the United States, water is H_2O: there are innumerable truths like this, which only idiots or obtuse academics (often thought to be the same thing) would deny. Sometimes it is hard to uncover the truth, but that is not because we don't understand what truth itself means. We may never know what happened to the *Mary Celeste* but there is a truth about it which if we did know would be plain and simple enough.

Even the dominant theories of truth in twentieth century Anglophone philosophy appeared simple to the point of banal. In the 1930s Alfred Tarski proposed: any statement 'P' is true if and only if P is true.[2] For example: 'Snow is white' if and only if snow is white. Blink and you might think this is an empty tautology, like saying 'black is black'. What saves it from vacuity is that 'P' in inverted commas is a linguistic statement while P without inverted commas is a truth about the world. Not quite empty then, and perhaps theoretically important, but hardly a game-changer for the everyday pursuer of truth.

Somehow, however, the truth has ceased to be plain or simple. Indeed, it is not uncommon to hear people deny that there is any such thing as the truth at all, only opinions, what is 'true-for-you' or 'true-for-me'. Scanning millions of books

3

and written texts, Google's N-Gram viewer reveals that the word 'truth' was used only a third as much at the turn of the millennium as it was 150 years previously. The decline in plain and simple truths is even more precipitous.

The problem is not that we lack a proper understanding of what 'truth' means. For practical purposes, it is hard to improve on Aristotle's early definition: 'To say of what is that it is not, or of what is not that it is, is false, while to say of what is that it is, and of what is not that it is not, is true.'[3] If that sounds obvious, if a bit cumbersome, perhaps it's because there's nothing mysterious about the ordinary meaning of truth. If there is a crisis of truth in the world today, the root of the problem is not the inadequacy of philosophical theories of truth. It can even be argued that in its dogged pursuit of truth, philosophy actually unleashed the sceptical forces that led to its being undermined. 'How do you know?' and 'What do you mean by ... ' are philosophers' questions that have been bastardised by a cynical society.

Introduction

Our problem is not primarily with what truth means but *how and by whom truth is established.* Truth used to seem simple because it was easy to assume that most of what we thought to be true really was true, that things were as they seemed, that the wisdom passed down the generations was timeless. This simplicity has been eroded by a variety of different forces. Science showed us that much of what we think about how the world works is false and that we are even mistaken about the workings of our own minds. The pace of its development has left us questioning whether today's orthodoxy will be tomorrow's outdated fallacy. In addition, the more the world shrinks through globalisation, the more we have reason to question whether what we take to be true in our cultures really is so or merely a local prejudice. The openness of democratic societies has also allowed the free press to expose more and more of what goes on in the corridors of power, making us more aware of the ways in which we are deceived. And the growth of psychology has enabled more people to master myriad techniques of manipulation, and more people to understand how they work, in a kind of arms race of deception in which truth is the main casualty.

Truth has become much less plain and simple, but I see no evidence at all that most people have ceased to believe in it. People remain as outraged by lies as they have ever done, which would make no sense if they did not believe they were untrue. Falsely accuse the most dedicated post-modernist that they have committed a crime and they will not shrug and accept that your version of events is just one narrative, a construction of reality that is as legitimate as any other. They may resist the language of truth in seminars but they will bite their tongues in court and swear to tell the truth, the whole truth, and nothing but the truth to defend themselves, knowing full well what that means and why it matters.

That's why talk of a 'post-truth' society is premature and misguided. The same data that shows a century-and-a-half decline in the use of the word 'truth' also points to a twenty-first-century revival in the concept. We wouldn't even be talking about post-truth if we didn't think truth mattered. The world is neither ready nor willing to say goodbye to truth, even in politics where it sometimes seems as though it has already taken its leave. The French philosopher Bernard-Henri Lévy is only half-right when he says 'The people listen less and less to policy and they even seem less concerned about whether the candidates are telling the truth or not.'[4] In fact, lies can still land politicians in very hot water indeed. Loss of interest in political truth is quite tightly focused on their policy promises and the evidence used to back them up. The electorate increasingly takes the view that manifesto commitments, supported by cherry-picked or invented facts and numbers, are not worth the paper they are no longer even printed on.

Underpinning this world-weary cynicism is a kind of defeatism, an acceptance that we do not have the resources to discern who's telling the truth and who's just trying it on. Feeling unable to distinguish truth from falsehood, electorates choose their politicians on other, more emotional factors. Losing trust in our brains, we tend to go with our guts and hearts instead.

The antidote is not a return to the comfort of simple truths. *The Plain Truth* disappeared in its original form, surely in part because it presented no such thing. It was the mouthpiece of an eccentric evangelical Christian sect led by its bullying, autocratic founder, Herbert W. Armstrong. Its promise of simple truth was seductive but false, like the pledges of populist politicians today. They tap into an understandable disenchantment with political elites and peddle the reassuring message that we don't need to listen to experts, only the will of the people. They promise a world that is not so much post-truth as post-complexity, and that is a powerful message in a disconcertingly uncertain world.

To rebuild belief in the power and value of truth, we can't dodge its complexity. Truths can be and often are difficult to understand, discover, explain, verify. They are also disturbingly easy to hide, distort, abuse or twist. Often we cannot claim with any certainty to know the truth. We need to take stock of the various kinds of real and supposed truths out there and understand how to test their authenticity. If we can do this then we might not be at the start of a post-truth era but rather at a temporary post-truth moment, a kind of cultural convulsion born of a despair that will give way in time to measured hope.

History and philosophy can be our guides, the former enabling us to see how the idea of truth has actually been used and abused, the latter helping us to see how it should ideally be. A neat, chronological history of truth would be a deeply untruthful one, since the concept has no such simple, linear biography. Our history instead jumps around the past, looking for events that best illustrate the complexities of truth, in order to understand the present and prepare for the future. Time and again we will find that the most telling episodes are where truth flirts with falsehood and vice-versa.

When devising my taxonomy of truths I turned not to philosophy textbooks but to what I judged to be the sources and justifications of truth-claims that were most important and problematic in real life. Each category illustrates how the means of legitimately establishing truth are imperfect and contain within them the potential for distortion. I hope to show that with honest intent and clarity of mind, we can guard against such misuse and see that the claim we live in a post-truth world is the most pernicious untruth of them all. It serves the interest of those who have the most to fear from the truth, plain and simple or not.

1. Eternal truths

Around 600 BCE, the prophet Lehi escaped Jerusalem shortly before its destruction and led his family with others to the Americas. His descendants formed a tribe of Israel, Lamanites, named after his son, from which other prophets emerged, writing down on gold plates in an unknown language the histories and powerful lessons they taught to their people. Around 400 CE, the last of these prophets, Moroni, buried the plates in what is now known as Wayne County in New York State. These lay hidden until on 21 September 1823 a prophet called Joseph Smith received a vision and by divine guidance was led the next day to the burial site. A year later, Moroni returned to Earth and led Smith back to the plates and three years after instructed Smith to translate them, using the divine gift of revelation. In 1830, the completed translation of *The Book of Mormon* went on sale in Palmyra, New York. It is the distinguishing sacred text for the Church of Jesus Christ of Latter Day Saints.

It is safe to say that at least 99.8 per cent of the world (the non-Mormon population) believes this story to be untrue. Not just false, but obviously, outrageously, ludicrously false. This is not because they all think that it is absurd to believe God revealed his truth to the world via specially selected human beings. Muslims believe that the *Qur'an* is the word of God, dictated to the prophet Mohammed by the angel Gabriel. Many Jews and Christians believe that God gave to Moses ten commandments carved on tablets of stone. The sacred texts of Hindus, the *Vedas*, are also believed by many to have been revealed to *rishis* (seers) by God.

There are many sacred texts which receive

much more respect than the *The Book of Mormon*. But there is not one that most people believe to be a genuine divine revelation. So the majority opinion about any given so-called revealed text is that it is not revealed at all. At the same time, many believe that one such text or set of texts is revealed. There is a wonderful paradox here: the majority does not accept majority opinion. In other words, a majority believes in at least one revelation that the majority judges to be false. This is a salutary lesson for anyone who trusts the wisdom of crowds.

The paradox persists, however, because it is not a true paradox at all. It is obviously not absurd or contradictory to take a minority position, and if of all the possible positions, none has majority support, a minority one has to be correct. That is what allows people to maintain the rationality of belief in their revelation (or lack of it), knowing full well most others reject it. The atheist position, which rejects all revelations, avoids the embarrassment of having to insist its holy book is different from all the others but at the price of insisting that the vast majority are wrong to think there is anything to this holiness game at all. Ultimately, it is just another minority view competing with all the rest.

What has this to do with the state of the 'post-truth' world? It is a reminder that many people still fervently believe not only in truths, but divinely given, eternal ones. One of the problems we face is not the absence of truth, but its overabundance. Competing eternal truths underpin many conflicts and divisions. After all, these supposedly revealed texts often contradict each other, meaning they are mutually incompatible. They can also get in the way of beliefs with a much greater claim to truth, such as when creationism leads to a rejection of evolution, one of the most established theories in science. Given these tensions created by revelation, in one respect the so-called 'fundamentalists' are rational in their fanaticism. It may be difficult to deny evolution or call your neighbour an idolater, but that is what the truth as they see it logically entails.

Fortunately, on the whole persistent belief in revealed truths has not been as divisive or as inimical to science as might have been expected. The majority of religious believers uphold the truth of their sacred texts while also accepting evolution, the big bang, quantum physics and other scientific theories. They are also generally sanguine about the beliefs of those who are faithful to other revelations. If intolerance and the rejection of science follows from literal belief in revelation we might conclude, by a kind of reverse inference, that when people tolerate others and accept science, they are not taking every word of their revelations to be literally true.

Is *that* true? Only if we give due weight to the 'every word' proviso in the proposition. It is very easy to fall into the trap of dividing believers into those who believe literally and those who do not. In fact few are either absolute literalists or happy to see the entirety of their faith as no more than metaphor and allegory. Most take a pick-and-mix attitude to literality, accepting some things as facts and others as just stories. Many Christians, for example, are not bothered whether Jesus really turned water into wine, unsure about all that business about post-mortem walking on water and appearing in a room with his disciples without going through the door, but convinced that Jesus was a historical figure whose resurrection is more than just a tall story with an important spiritual message.

Even when believers lean towards the more literalist end of the spectrum, many find it surprisingly easy to combine acceptance of modern science with historical science-defying miracles. There is a strong tradition in Islam, for example, of insisting that nothing in the *Qur'an* contradicts science and there are many ways of interpreting the text to maintain such compatibility. With ingenuity, belief in occasional divine intervention and extraordinary events in the past can sit alongside belief in the findings of science. Maintaining that God can ignore the laws of physics is compatible with accepting that on all other occasions those laws hold.

Moreover, among those with fewer commitments to the literal truth of doctrine, few go the whole hog and accept their stories and creeds are *mere* metaphors. Sacred texts may not always be historical records but for believers they contain genuine, profound truths. To say Jesus is the son of God, for example, is not to say the almighty impregnated Mary but neither is it just a figure of speech. Clearly articulating the supposed truth here is extremely difficult — and that is precisely the point. To be religious is to accept that there is a divine mind beyond human comprehension, so of course our own understanding will be limited and partial by comparison. Rather than insist on pinning truth down, the most rational thing for the religious to do is accept that faith is somewhat mysterious. The most essential truths for the believer can become not so much facts about the cosmos but insights into how we ought to live, ways of orienting ourselves towards the transcendent.

Religion does not just promote different truths, it advocates different *grounds of truth*.

The truth of religion is something many believers feel almost viscerally. It connects to their very sense of self, identity and belonging. It is as much, or more, *felt* than *thought*.

The impatient atheist finds all this evasive. The modern, scientific outlook is one in which you could make a list of purported facts about the world and tick them off as true, false, or unknown. And you certainly don't do this on the basis of feelings, no matter how strongly felt. This seems simple enough but when it comes to the truths people live by, history has taught us that this is just not how it works.

There are many atheists who believe that it would be progress simply to eliminate all belief in revealed truths. But trying too hard to make religion extinct is likely to be counter-productive, as well as unnecessary. Fundamentalism is problematic but as we have seen, even some forms of literalism can accommodate themselves with secular truth, however uncomfortably.

Ideally, both atheist and believer alike would agree that any religious truths worthy of the name are of a distinctive variety. They may be more than mere fictions, but they do not belong to the list of objective facts about the world, alongside the atomic weight of gold or the date of the first Moon landings. No one should mistake theology for science, myth for history. If any eternal truths exist, what should make them special is that they are not of the ordinary, empirical kind. Ironically, those who treat them as such diminish rather than defend their faiths.

This is one of many reasons why lovers of the truth should avoid talking of 'The Truth'. Religion and secular knowledge clash when both see themselves as offering competing realities. When they accept that their truths are of different species, coexistence is possible. We should be encouraged by the fact that many theologians agree with this diagnosis, even if too much of what they go on to say contradicts it. The spread of this understanding of religious truth, rather than shrinking religious faith, offers our best hope of reducing religion as a source of conflict in the world.

2. Authoritative truths

Sathya Sai Baba claimed to be a living God who could make objects like *vibhuti* (holy ash), jewellery and watches materialise, cure the sick and see the future. Having predicted that he would live in good health before dying at the age of 96, he died in 2011 when he was 84, having spent most of the previous seven years in a wheelchair. His followers included the cricket legend Sachin Tendulkar, founder of Hard Rock Cafe Isaac Tigrett, the jazz musician Alice Coltrane and the Indian Prime Minister Atal Bihari Vajpayee. At the time of writing, the Sathya Sai Organisation he founded still has over 1,000 branches in more than 100 countries.

Sai Baba is not a one-off. India has always had numerous *swamis* or *gurus* with large followings, many of whom are widely believed to be tricksters and charlatans. Outsiders are baffled as to how people like Sai Baba can gain such credence. But reliance on the insight of authorities, and the authority of our insight, is in fact historically ubiquitous.

To understand why anyone is taken to be an epistemic authority – an authority on truth – it is vital to understand what authorises them. It's sometimes tempting to see such authority as self-generated, a personality cult created by the charisma of the individual. But not even the most persuasive orator or media performer can get people to believe anything. Their supposed authority always comes stamped by some kind of seal.

The two most common validators of epistemological authority are expertise or the divine. To take the last first, when the white smoke emerges from the Vatican, the Holy Spirit is thought to have ensured that the right candidate

22

has been elected as Pope. Similar beliefs about the divine hand govern the choice of other religious leaders. Indeed, for much of European history, monarchs too were thought to have been chosen by God, as were the aristocracy. Some church congregations still sing the verse of the hymn 'All Things Bright and Beautiful' which says, 'The rich man in his castle, the poor man at his gate. God made them high and lowly and ordered their estate.'

Like it or not, such divine authority still commands wide respect. Those worried about it cannot wish it away or hope to persuade billions around the world that no such authority exists. They are nonetheless entitled to protest if those who claim the mandate of heaven try to assert authority beyond the theological, talking not only of the eternal truths we looked at in the last chapter but of secular truths that are settled by those who study the world rather than the heavens.

However, few today claim to speak directly on behalf of the divine, expecting people to be satisfied with that. Even in religion, authority usually rests on some claim to expertise. Sai Baba, for instance, gained his authority by claims to a kind of spiritual expertise, manifested in his miracles and clairvoyance. Any claims he made to be speaking the word of God were taken to be reliable because of this expertise.

The very idea of 'spiritual expertise' may strike some as bizarre, but not to those who live in a culture wherein many (but by no means all) people believe that the world is fundamentally the same as the one of innumerable deities and miracles described in the ancient *Vedas*. The idea of spiritual excellence is no stranger in India than that of sporting prowess is everywhere, and in both cases it is accepted that one can attain it by a combination of effort and giftedness, in varying proportions.

Secular expertise also grants authority, as indicated by the fact that experts are often described as leading authorities on their subjects. No one thinks this odd and for good reason.

There are many things of which most of us know very little and understand even less, so we accept we have to defer to the authority of experts. Those who believe this is rational but that it is foolish to defer to the authority of spiritual experts have no quarrel with the principle of deference to authority per se.

The question is when is it right to accept (or at least give weight to) an authority's version of the truth? To decide this we need a kind of epistemological triage. First we ask, is this a domain in which *anyone* can speak truth? If we do not believe in anything supernatural or in key tenets of a spiritual tradition, we won't take anyone speaking on these matters to be an authority. Scepticism about any given supposed authority is hence often secondary to scepticism about what that authority speaks on. Gurus are dismissed by many not because there is evidence of their *particular* fraudulence or delusion, but because it is assumed there is no truth in *anything* they claim to talk about.

If we believe there are truths to be known,

the second stage of triage is to ask what kind of expert is a trustworthy source of truth in that domain. Take health. We all assume there are truths to be told about it, but we also know that many different disciplines exist that claim to offer it: doctors, herbalists, chiropractors, Reiki healers. Again, if we have good reason to dismiss any of these then we can dismiss any particular practitioner without needing to give them a personal assessment.

If we allow truth can be said about something and that there are experts on it, we can conduct the final stage of triage. Then, and only then is our question about whether a *particular* expert is to be trusted. This triage has to take account of the fact that not all expert views are equal. If my electrician warns me that touching a wire will electrocute me, I have no reason to doubt her. If a doctor tells me I should lose a little weight, my knowledge of the incomplete state of nutritional science might justify at least a little hesitancy. If my doctor is a trained physician but a known maverick, we need to be even more careful. If one economist predicts there will be no recession in the coming year, it might be sensible not to do anything differently at all as a result.

This triage allows for different judgements at every stage, which helps explain why some people who seem obviously to be charlatans or dreamers are taken by many to be experts. If you find yourself bemused by this seeming gullibility, it is often because you start with an assumption either that there is no such expertise for them to have (stage one triage) or that they belong to a school of thought with no legitimacy (stage two). These are assumptions that believers don't share and it is not straightforward to show why they should. Swamis might seem absurd to you but there are spiritual authorities in other religions all around the world. Homeopathy might also seem crushed by the weight of scientific evidence but many sincere, intelligent people who know more about health than the average layman still advocate it.

Every culture accepts some people as authorities. Truth becomes a victim of this only when such authority is either unwarranted or exceeds its scope. It is unwarranted when there are either no truths to be had or someone is in no position to claim special knowledge of them. It exceeds its scope when people are taken as authorities on matters outside of their expertise. So, for example, no one is an authority on Reiki healing because it doesn't work and so there are no truths to be learned about *how* it works. And scientists don't have any authority to give the last word on the ethics of their science because their expertise is scientific rather than ethical.

The principle that authority must be warranted and not exceed its scope is simple enough, but putting it into practice is extremely difficult. I confidently just asserted that Reiki doesn't work. I almost used homeopathy as an example but chose the softer target to reduce the volume of inevitable angry correspondence I get whenever I point out the absence of good evidence that certain alternative medicines work. The response is to be expected because some people reject the authority of medical scientists and accept that of homeopaths. Furthermore they accept no superior third kind of authority that can settle the dispute, certainly not a philosopher.

This sums up beautifully the core problem of truth by authority. We *need* to defer to experts but not everyone who claims to be an expert is one. If we decide which experts to defer to on the basis of expert opinion, we paradoxically have to choose which experts to trust in order to decide which experts to trust. So inevitably our choice of experts is at bottom based on our own judgement, even though we know that it is not fully informed. In other words, we accept the authority of our own judgement in order to decide whose authority of judgement to accept.

There is no way out of this. Reason's dirty secret is that we have to rely on our own judgement without being able rationally to justify it completely. This is not a counsel of despair. By attending to justifications and evidence we can minimise the role of our own insight and maximise the role of facts, evidence and sound inference. But we shouldn't kid ourselves we can rely solely on logically following the facts.

Getting the balance right between our own judgement and the expert testimony of others is difficult, and the post-truth world doesn't try too hard to walk the tightrope. Our current predicament is that authorities of expertise are routinely dismissed, with the authority of the gut, intuition, the people and/or God taking its place. There is not enough emphasis given to the wisdom of genuine experts who have devoted their lives to the study of their subjects. This is not a completely different world to a more rational one, simply one where things have become unbalanced. If we care about the truth, we can neither reject nor too enthusiastically embrace the authorities who appear to guide us towards it. Rather, we have to take more care as to whom we grant authority, and on what basis.

But we cannot escape the exercise of our own woefully under-informed judgement. That is what lies behind Kant's Enlightenment injunction '*sapere aude!*'.[5] Dare to know. And daring it is, because it always carries the risk of error. Don't think *by* yourself but do think *for* yourself, not because you're wiser or smarter than other people but because ultimately that's what you have to do. No one can make up your mind for you, unless you make up your mind to let them.

3. Esoteric truths

We all know what happened in New York City on 9/11, 2001. At least, we all know *some* of what happened. Two planes crashed into the twin towers of the World Trade Center, both of which subsequently caught fire and eventually collapsed, killing 2,763 people. Not everyone, however, sees this sequence of events as one of cause and effect. For many in the so-called 9/11 truth movement, the impact of the planes does not account for the towers' collapse. They believe that the whole thing was staged by the CIA as a pretence to launch a war in the Middle East and that the towers were brought down by explosives in a controlled demolition.

These 'truthers', as they are pejoratively known, are widely dismissed by the vast majority of the general public as well as by experts in fields from espionage to civil engineering. They are lumped together with other deranged conspiracy theorists, such as those who think that the Moon landings were faked in a film studio, that the Holocaust never happened, or that the world is controlled by a secret society called the Illuminati, who may or may not be lizard-like aliens who have taken human form.

The truthers are almost certainly wrong, but simply dismissing them with condescending laughter is misguided. Conspiracy theories persist not because people are crazy, but because some truths are, and have always been, hidden. It takes careful thought to avoid the Scylla of complacently accepting the official version of truth and the Charybdis of paranoically believing implausible alternatives.

The idea that some truths are hidden, or 'esoteric', is as old as human civilisation. In Ancient Greece, it is widely believed that in addition to

the exoteric teachings that philosophers advo-
cated publicly, there were secret esoteric teachings
that were only revealed to an inner circle. The
idea that the Pythagoreans had secret teachings,
for example, was undisputed. It is only fairly
recently, in fact, that scholars have tended to
assume that Plato did not have esoteric as well as
exoteric teachings.

Some esoterica is not merely hidden, it is dis-
guised by wilful deception. In Plato's *Republic*,
Socrates advocates telling the masses a made-up
creation story which explains why everyone
belongs to a particular social class and has a duty
to protect the motherland from which they came.
If people believed this myth, Socrates claimed it
'would have a good effect, making them more
inclined to care for the state and one another'.

This is often cited as the original 'noble lie', a
falsehood propagated to serve a higher goal.
Sometimes, however, the purpose of such lies is
no more than self-interest. Hence Machiavelli is
widely quoted as advising an ambassador, 'Occa-
sionally words must serve to veil the facts. But

let this happen in such a way that no one become aware of it; or, if it should be noticed, excuses must be at hand to be produced immediately.' (Ironically, this is an example of what it describes, since it significantly *misquotes* Machiavelli's original, perhaps to add legitimacy to the idea of the noble lie or to cast Machiavelli as more of an amoralist than he actually was.)

'Conspiracy theorists' therefore make two entirely correct assumptions: that important truths are sometimes hidden, often behind deliberate lies, and that those who do the hiding usually do so to protect their own interests. You don't need to be much of a cynic to add that people who have an interest in keeping the truth esoteric will do so if they possibly can. That is the moral of Plato's parable of the magical Ring of Gyges, which makes its wearer invisible. Socrates's foil in the dialogue, Glaucon, contends that no one who wore such a ring 'can be imagined to be of such an iron nature that he would stand fast in justice'. He would steal what he wanted and 'sleep with any one at his pleasure'.[6] A lie can likewise cloak our villainy so as to make it practically invisible. You don't have to believe that all humans would take advantage of such an invisibility cloak to believe that many would.

That is why some conspiracy theories turn out to be true. One of the most famous is that the CIA manipulated the American media. While it never controlled all of it, in the sixties and seventies there was indeed a CIA Operation Mockingbird that spied on members of the Washington press corps and paid journalists to publish CIA propaganda.

One state-sponsored conspiracy theory also turned out to have some truth in it. The McCarthyite 'Red Scare' led to many innocent people being falsely accused of 'un-American' (i.e. communist) activities. However, it later transpired that there were indeed a significant number of Soviet spies and informants in the Roosevelt and Truman administrations, and that a number of people accused by McCarthy were indeed guilty as charged.

These examples, while rare, show that it is not enough to identify something as a conspiracy theory to dismiss it. Anyone concerned with the truth needs to have a way of distinguishing between plausible and implausible plots.

The problem is that most people don't have the time or knowledge to work out which is which. Take the 9/11 truthers. Common sense supports their assertion that planes flying into the tops of skyscrapers would not cause them to collapse all of a sudden from a point lower than the impact. To understand why they are wrong, you need to have specialised knowledge of engineering, or to trust those who do. Most of us have little choice but to take the latter option.

But trust in authorities is at an all-time low. As the Italian comedian turned politician Beppe Grillo put it, 'the amateurs are the ones conquering the world and I'm rejoicing in it because the professionals are the ones who have reduced the world to this state.'[7] This dismissal of experts in not entirely irrational. Experts have been wrong on a number of very significant things:

the relative unhealthiness of fat and sugar, the dangers presented to the world's computers by the 'millennium bug', the presence of weapons of mass destruction in Iraq, the robustness of the world's financial markets, the advantages of adopting a common currency in the Eurozone, and so on. Experts are far from infallible.

Hence in the early twenty-first century we find ourselves in a position where we know some truths are hidden by powerful groups to protect their own interests, we are not usually competent enough judges to know which claims about such esoteric truths are correct, and we don't have much confidence in experts to make those judgements for us. Is it any wonder that more and more of us are willing to believe that important truths are being hidden from us, despite an absence of strong — or sometimes *any* — evidence? After all, even the *lack* of evidence is entirely explicable: if truths are successfully hidden, so is much of the evidence for them.

Step back, however, and it is clear that this has

gone too far. When even an elected president can make entirely unsubstantiated claims of clandestine vote-rigging and phone-tapping without shame or fear of serious censure, belief in esoteric truths has become too widespread. The distinction between paranoia and justified suspicion has become dangerously blurred.

The problem is in part a failure to appreciate that having good reason to believe there are numerous concealed truths is not a reason to believe most claims to have uncovered them. Any number of things we assume to be true could be false because someone is deceiving us. But in the absence of good evidence that something is being hidden, it is rash to assume that it is. We don't start digging for buried treasure in any random spot and nor should we start digging for buried truths on the basis of rumour, hunch or unjustified assertion.

Our scepticism needs to be mitigated and there is no better model for how to do this than the Scottish philosopher David Hume, who combined a rigorous scepticism with a good nose for baloney. Hume offers the simple maxim 'A wise man proportions his belief to the evidence.'[8] To take seriously any claim about esoteric truths we need a good reason to believe its veracity, not merely a suspicion of those accused of hiding them. Where evidence is existent but weak, we should proportion our beliefs by accepting that the claim is plausible while in the meantime adopting an 'innocent until proven guilty' principle.

Often there is no cost to suspending judgement. The philosopher Jay Kennedy, for example, claims to have discovered the key to unlocking the esoteric teachings in Plato's dialogues.[9] He has yet to persuade most of his colleagues, but we should not read too much into this. There is a difference between saying something other experts do not yet see a reason to endorse and saying something that other experts have strong grounds to believe is definitely false. Not knowing how to judge the evidence, we can sit back and let history decide. Kennedy does not belong in the same camp as 9/11 truthers because nothing he says implies either mass deception or collective stupidity among his peers.

One of the perennial challenges of being a critical thinker is to be appropriately sceptical without being indiscriminately cynical. When we slide from the former to the latter we swap one form of gullibility for another, from being too willing to buy the official line to too quick to accept any alternative to it. To return conspiracy theories to the margins of culture, away from the centre-ground they now occupy, therefore requires no more than a recalibration of our sceptical faculties. We need to row back on our cynicism without in any way decreasing our scepticism.

4. Reasoned truths

In 1804, Thomas Jefferson expressed the hope that the United States of America had embarked on an experiment that 'we trust will end in establishing the fact, that man may be governed by reason and truth.'[10] The announcement by Oxford Dictionaries 212 years later that 'post-truth' was its Word of the Year seemed to confirm that the experiment had failed.

When experiments don't work, scientists do not usually completely abandon the hypothesis they are testing. Rather, they review their methods or assumptions to figure out what they have got wrong, tweak the experiment and try again. Similarly, those analysing the effects of placing reason and truth at the centre of government should not give up yet. Perhaps we have been testing the wrong things.

There is one model of rationality that experience should tell us to now abandon. There is a long tradition in Western philosophy of seeing reason as a potential generator of absolute truths, a kind of logic machine into which we could feed indubitable facts and first principles, and out of which would come a complete understanding.

In modern philosophy, the two great representatives of this optimistic 'rationalist' tradition were René Descartes and Baruch Spinoza. Both were impressed by the ways in which proofs were generated in mathematics and geometry. They thought that with due care and diligence, it would be possible to replicate this precision in all areas of human knowledge. 'Those long chains composed of very simple and easy reasonings, which geometers customarily use to arrive at their most difficult demonstrations,' wrote Descartes, 'had given me occasion to suppose that all the things which come within the scope of human knowledge are interconnected in the same way.'[11]

While Descartes tried to emulate these methods, Spinoza explicitly attempted to copy them. In his magnum opus, *The Ethics*, he broke down the elements of his arguments into definitions, axioms, propositions, corollaries and proofs, trying to make each step follow inexorably from the preceding one. Applying this method, by the third page he already felt confident enough to conclude, without any empirical observations at all, let alone particle accelerators or electron microscopes, that 'Every substance is necessarily infinite.'[12] His proof was entirely *a priori*, from pure reason, without the complications of experimental evidence.

For the rationalists, reason is superior to observation because it can get behind mere appearances, the world as given to the senses, and see with certainty reality as it truly is. 'Reason perceives this necessity of things truly, i.e., as it is in itself,' wrote Spinoza. For him, the reward was nothing less than a God's eye view of the world. 'It is of the nature of Reason to regard things *sub specie aeternitatis* (under the aspect of eternity).'[13]

While there are still some die-hard rationalists left, even they have mostly abandoned Descartes' and Spinoza's more ambitious claims for the power of reason. Most philosophers would agree with the physicist Werner Heisenberg's words: 'It will never be possible by pure reason to arrive at some absolute truth.'[14]

David Hume worked out the basic flaw in rationalism back in the eighteenth century. All pure reason could analyse was the relationship between concepts. But this tells us nothing about the relationship between the things in the world those concepts relate to. '1+1=2' is a truth about numbers, but says nothing about what happens when you put two physical things together, where they might annihilate each other, merge into one, or multiply.

Despite rationalism's decline, the idea has persisted that the highest form of reason is logical in structure, like the deductions of geometers. The closer we bring our reasoning to this form, the more 'rigorous' and 'robust' it is. The psychologists Hugo Mercier and Dan Sperber have described succinctly what is wrong with this view. In order to make our arguments logical, we have to simplify them, stripping out all the ambiguity, vagueness and complexity so as to be able to express them in logical forms such as 'If x, then y'. This does not so much *reveal* the logical relations between our assumptions as *exaggerate* them, creating an illusion of clarity that disguises the truth that 'there are no adequate instructions for reasoning effectively about most real life problems.'[15]

This isn't reason at its best, but reason at its purest. Like alcohol, when it is too pure, reason becomes unpalatable and potentially toxic. Reason works best in a blend which includes not just logic but experience, evidence, judgement, subtlety of thought, and sensitivity to ambiguity. Reason in its broader and most practical sense is essentially the capacity to make inferences, on the basis of sound reasons. But we make these inferences in many ways, and the deductive logic beloved of rationalists is not the main one.[16]

A more modest idea of reason, and our power to use it, would help us to avoid becoming too confident in the rationality and truth of our own beliefs. Despite the fact that intelligent people evidently disagree, we are inclined to think that what *we* believe really is rational and that those who disagree are being blinded by prejudices, ignorance or plain stupidity. Like Descartes, we become confident that we see things are true by the 'pure light of reason'.[17] But the light of reason is never pure and even when it does shine clearly, we often go wrong because we only see what is directly under it, not what lies elsewhere in the dark.

When taking reason down a peg or two, however, we must be careful not to go too far. People often mistake the exposing of reason's limitations with its debunking. Armed with evidence from psychology that most of our thinking is done automatically and quickly by 'hot' emotion-laden processes, rather than consciously and slowly by the cool intellect, too many dismiss reason as merely a tool for after-the-event justification. Humans, on this view, are not rational but rationalisers, not acting on good reasons but finding reasons retrospectively.[18]

The most reasonable view of reason neither elevates it too high nor drags it down too low. Reason is an imperfect tool with imperfect users. We should indeed strive to be as rational as we can be and to proportion our confidence in the truth of beliefs. But that proportioning requires a realistic view of how confident we can ever be. Reason does not lead us to the truth, if only we obediently follow it. It is more like a navigation tool that can help us get closer to the truth, if we know how to use it, and what we're looking for.

Ironically, the evidence that we can indeed be rational enough is intimately connected with exactly the same evidence for the everyday weakness of reason. The way in which we discovered the differences between hot, automatic processes and cool, calm reason was by rational, scientific investigation, with incredible results. Only by using reason could we discover our own cognitive flaws. It's a smart creature that understands very well the nature of its own stupidity. And understanding the traps of irrationality we fall into means we can become better at avoiding them.

5. Empirical truths

The English Renaissance philosopher, states-
man and scientist Francis Bacon is widely
credited with establishing the fundamentals of
the experimental method in science. 'The best
demonstration by far is experience, if it go not
beyond the actual experiment,' he wrote in his
Novum Organum.[19] Bacon showed in words how
science proceeds by trial and error, and in deed
how some of its errors prove to be fatal. Travel-
ling by coach and horse with one of the king's
physicians to Highgate in London, it suddenly
occurred to Bacon that the snow lying all around
him might be as effective as salt at preserving
flesh. Desiring to test the theory without delay,

the pair went into a poor woman's house at the bottom of Highgate Hill, bought a hen off her which they got her to eviscerate, and then stuffed it with snow. In the process, however, Bacon caught such a sudden and extreme chill that he couldn't even make it home. The Earl of Arundel, who lived locally, put him up but unfortunately in a damp bed that did more harm than good. A few days later he died of pneumonia.

Given that Bacon helped establish the empirical principle that conclusions should be grounded in evidence, it is ironic that this well-known story about him is probably apocryphal.[20] The irony, however, goes deeper than that. Bacon's supposed cause of death exemplifies the difficulties of taking a scientific, evidence-based approach in the first place. Folk wisdom has for centuries insisted that it is possible to 'catch a chill'. But when modern science examined the evidence for this, it seemed to be no more than an old-wives' tale. A number of laboratory experiments introduced cold viruses into people's noses, exposing some to cold air and others not, and they repeatedly showed that the temperature had no effect at all.[21] The reason for this seemed simple enough: the common cold is caused by rhinoviruses, flu by influenza viruses, pneumonia by a bacteria. Temperature has nothing to do with it. If you get extremely cold for too long you can get hypothermia, but you can't 'catch a chill'.

Then in January 2015, headlines like 'Mom Was Right: You'll Catch a Cold from Being Cold' appeared in serious newspapers and magazines. A team at Yale University led by Ellen F. Foxman had found that 'the innate immune response to the rhinovirus is impaired at the lower body temperature compared to the core body temperature.'[22] In other words, whether the cold virus is present in your nose does not depend on the temperature, but your immune response to it does, and that means you may indeed be more likely to catch a cold if you get cold: or rather, more likely to *hatch* a cold if your nose has already caught the virus.

These examples don't look like good evidence for the reliability of evidence-based truth. We are left without enough evidence to reach firm and final conclusions both on an historical question about the cause of a particular death and a scientific question about causes of deaths in general. We seek evidence but often, perhaps usually, it is elusive, absent, ambiguous, inconclusive. Etymologically, empirical means 'from experience', and experience seems to be telling us that an empirical approach leaves us with uncertainty, rather than knowledge.

Far from being a weakness, however, the open-endedness of empirical enquiry is actually its strength. David Hume made this point wonderfully when he observed that 'all the objects of human reason or enquiry may naturally be divided into two kinds, to wit, Relations of Ideas, and Matters of Fact.'[23] Relations of ideas concern truths of maths, geometry and pure logic. As we have seen, such truths are, in effect, true by definition, but they tell us nothing about the real world. Matters of fact, in contrast, cannot be established by pure logic. That also means they cannot be established with 100 per cent certainty. 'The contrary of every matter of fact is still possible,' warned Hume. 'That the sun will not rise to-morrow is no less intelligible a proposition, and implies no more contradiction than the affirmation, that it will rise.' Indeed, we can easily imagine circumstances in which we would have to accept that the sun is unlikely to rise tomorrow, such as if a massive asteroid were about to hit the Earth.

A lack of certainty is therefore part of the deal with empirical truth. We need to give up on it in order to take up the possibility of knowledge of the world. Absolute certainties can only be obtained about purely conceptual matters, such as axioms of mathematics and laws of logic. If we want to know about the world then there is potentially no end of discoveries – for ourselves or the entire human race – that might force us to alter our opinions. (That's why despite my best efforts, it is almost inevitable that I have unintentionally stated at least one falsehood in this book.) What we hold to be true is constantly open to being tested, which makes the truths that pass the test more reliable. The strength of empirical truth resides in the fact that it is always open to scrutiny, revision and rejection.

It needs to be stressed that the empiricist principle of experience being the arbiter of truth should not be confused with the fallacy that seeing is believing. I trust all sorts of things I know about the world on the basis of scientific experiments I have not witnessed, much more than I do some things that seem to have clearly happened before my very eyes. I've seen a human being sawn in two. I have no idea how it was done but I know it was an illusion. Nor does the mere addition of other witnesses necessarily make for a stronger empirical case. In 1983 millions of television viewers saw the illusionist David Copperfield make the Statue of Liberty 'disappear' but of course he did no such thing. 'Data' is not the plural of 'anecdote', as scientists are fond of saying. The basis of our truth claims therefore needs to be the totality of evidence relevant to the case, not just the evidence that is most evident to us at the time, no matter how many of 'us' there are.

One of the first philosophers to appreciate the importance of evidence was Aristotle. In his *Ethics*, he wrote that 'the solution of a difficulty consists in the discovery of facts'.[24] He was right, but like many since he did not perhaps appreciate how difficult it is to discover all the facts that will resolve a difficulty once and for all. Bacon was more realistic, recognising that new facts come up against the resistance of prejudice, assumptions and prior beliefs. 'No one has yet been found so firm of mind and purpose as resolutely to compel himself to sweep away all theories and common notions, and to apply the understanding, thus made fair and even, to a fresh examination of particulars,' he wrote. 'Thus it happens that human knowledge, as we have it, is a mere medley and ill-digested mass, made up of much credulity and much accident, and also of the childish notions which we at first imbibed.'[25]

Proponents of evidence-based truth need to recognise these obstacles and the difficulty of establishing sufficiently strong evidence so as to make a case effectively conclusive. People who deny anthropogenic climate change, for example, are not simply uninterested in evidence. Rather, they have learned the wrong lessons about the fallibility of scientific modelling and prediction so miscalculate the probability that human activity is dangerously warming the planet. Indeed, it would be against the spirit of empirical enquiry to insist that these 'deniers' are simply and certainly wrong. They could be right. The objection can be no stronger than that the balance of evidence is heavily against them, and this is as strong as any objection can be.

However, too many proponents of empirical truth talk as though it were simpler than this. They like stirring *cris de cœur* (or perhaps that should be *cris de cerveau*) like Baron D'Holbach's 1770 pronouncement that 'If error and ignorance have forged the chains which bind people in oppression, if it is prejudice which perpetuates those chains, science, reason and truth will one day be able to break them.'[26] Evidence rarely provides a single, decisive, emancipatory break with error. It is more like a flow of water that can sometimes wash all before it away, but more often slowly carves the landscape, eroding the hard rock that stands in its way.

The successes of modern science, including the tremendous advances in medicine, are owed to the judicious use of empirical methods. To deny this has expanded our store of truths because empirical knowledge is never 100 per cent certain would be to make a demand of truth that it could never conceivably meet. Empirical truth is too modest to claim certainty and is all the more admirable for it.

6. Creative truths

In 2005, President George W. Bush stood on the deck of USS *Abraham Lincoln* and declared 'mission accomplished' in Iraq. Well, not quite. Bush never uttered those words, which were actually displayed on a huge banner draped across the ship. He did, however, say that 'Iraq is free', that 'We've begun the search for hidden chemical and biological weapons', and that 'We will stand with the new leaders of Iraq as they establish a government of, by, and for the Iraqi people'. Many now see these as lies, or at least falsehoods. So with the benefit of hindsight, were Bush's words true or false?

The question risks misunderstanding the

nature of such declarations. Bush was never simply describing the facts: he was declaring both his hopes and intentions. As his promise of support indicated, no one was so naïve as to believe the job was literally over, so that everyone could go home and leave behind a liberated nation. Iraq's freedom depended on continued assistance. His words only make sense if they are taken to be as much about what *was* to happen as what *had already* happened.

It was not the first time that a statement of intent by Bush was mistaken for a description of facts. When he told the world, before a joint session of Congress eleven days after 9/11, 'Either you are with us, or you are with the terrorists', he was not stating a fact but issuing an ultimatum. This was made clear by the sentence that preceded it, usually omitted when it is quoted: 'Every nation, in every region, now has a decision to make.' Bush wasn't *stating* a fact, he was *creating* one. By saying that nations were either with him or against him, he was making it true.

The idea that you can make something true just by saying it strikes many as just the kind of nonsense the post-truth world has led us to. In fact, it is not at all mysterious how saying can make it so. When a legally sanctioned celebrant says, 'I now declare you husband and wife', a legal union is sealed. And when a Muslim man says to his wife *'talāq'* three times, then in some jurisdictions at least, he divorces her. These are examples of what the philosopher J. L. Austin called illocutionary speech acts, when 'by saying something, we *do* something'.[27] It is because some speech acts are illocutionary that it is not an infringement of free speech to prohibit incitement: calling on people to inflict harm on others is part of what *causes* that harm.

Just as words can change truths, new truths can change words. Where same-sex couples can be wed, the meaning of 'marriage' has been changed, creating new truths about what is required to be married. Truths are being created all the time, changing reality for better or for worse. Truths about economic inequality are not brute facts of nature, they are created by political decisions. 'Facts on the ground' are changed by construction, bombing, public policy.

Truth only becomes a victim of our creativity when we are not so much creating as confabulating. Saying is often not enough to make it so, and too often the assertion of a truth fails to weaken the obstinacy of reality. This is what was objectionable about the claim by Karl Rove, an advisor to George W. Bush, in 2004 that 'We're an empire now, and when we act, we create our own reality.'[28] In one way, this was simply stating the obvious. Every time the US acted in Iraq, which was what Rove was discussing with the journalist who quoted him, it did indeed change reality. But Rove appeared to cross a line when he dismissed the likes of journalists as living 'in what we call the reality-based community'. The remark appeared to betray a hubris, that the world could be divided between those who observed 'discernible reality' and those who created it. What Rove underestimated, and history suggested the Bush administration misunderestimated,[29] was how important it was accurately to discern existing reality first if you intend to change it. Not just any truth can be created.

Creativity requires imagination but in order to create new truths, imagination is not enough. Being 'creative with the truth' is no more than a euphemism for not telling the truth at all. But because truth can indeed be created — sometimes merely by saying the right thing at the right time — it is not always easy to distinguish those who are creating truth and those who are creatively hiding or disfiguring it. Indeed, sometimes there is a grey area between the two, one that dissemblers exploit.

Perhaps the most notorious recent example is Donald Trump's advocacy of 'truthful hyperbole' which he calls 'an innocent form of exaggeration', a 'very effective form of promotion'. There is some *prima facie* plausibility to this. Exaggeration is a kind of natural social lubricant. People embellish anecdotes to make them more interesting, talk up their strengths in order to get jobs, praise others excessively to ingratiate themselves to them or just to make others feel better. Could not such 'white lies' just as easily be called 'grey truths', neither completely true nor false?

No. Some lies are indeed harmless, even beneficial, but it is very important we do not confuse them with truths. Trump must know that whatever 'truthful hyperbole' is, it isn't really truthful at all. He himself said that its purpose is to 'play to people's fantasies', their desire 'to believe that something is the biggest and the greatest and the most spectacular'. But indulging a fantasy is neither truthful nor usually harmless, as Tony Schwartz, the ghost writer of Trump's *The Art of the Deal* now acknowledges. He disowns the now notorious passage, saying deceit is never innocent. ' "Truthful hyperbole" is a contradiction in terms. It's a way of saying, "It's a lie, but who cares?" '[30]

Recognising the myriad ways in which truth can be created gives us cause to be optimistic about the future. It also gives us tools to respond to attempts to create new truths we don't like. In politics, people are always being accused of lying, but unless they are very dumb indeed, few politicians tell brazen lies. That means the debate gets stuck at name-calling, the play-ground rhetoric of 'pants on fire'. Sometimes, rather than disputing versions of past events, it is more fruitful to focus on what truths are try-ing to be created. Past truths cannot be undone, but future ones are not yet set in stone.

7. Relative truths

The anthropologist Franz Boas is responsible for releasing the meme that the Inuit have many words for snow, a factoid that has spread all over the world, eventually settling on a lexical count of fifty.[31] A later, less virulent but still vigorous counter-meme is that the 'Eskimo words for snow' story is in fact an urban myth. Which is correct? The clever (but not necessarily wise) answer would be 'It depends what you mean by "true".' There is a certain aptness to this fudge because the fifty words for snow meme is one of the most common examples used to defend the idea that no truth is absolute, all are relative.

Recall the correspondence theory of truth which states that ' "Snow is white" is true if and only if snow is white.' The relativist can very easily puncture the apparent simplicity and obviousness of this by pointing out that it is not at all given what 'snow' or even 'white' is. At the last count, the Dulux paint range contained thirty-two different whites, from chalky, through cotton to handkerchief. ('Snow' was not one of them, perhaps because you'd first have to specify which of the fifty types the colour was supposed to match.) Relativism finds its way in here because it would seem clear that we can't even identify and count the varieties of things without taking on a cultural perspective. The relativist argues there are no *bare facts* only *interpretations of facts*, mediated through culture. Nothing is true, period; it is only true for certain people, in certain contexts, or in certain senses.

Once the relativism genie is out of the bottle it can take on almost any shape. It would be odd, after all, if there were fifty kinds of snow and only one of relativism. Truth can be relative to cultures, sub-cultures, epochs, ethnic groups, sexes, genders, social classes and even ultimately the individual. 'My truth' and 'true for you' now often trump claims to any objective standard. To disagree with someone risks contravening their right to a personal truth. Truth has become personalised, with the individual sovereign over their own interpretation of reality.

For many scientists and anglophone philosophers this is all too much. 'Relativism is the first refuge of the scoundrel,' writes Roger Scruton.[32] Relativism has become a *bête-noir* partly because in the broader culture, the sloppiest variety has taken hold. In philosophy, ideas concerning what is often called relativism (not always by those propounding them) are used to question established versions of the truth and power structures in careful, thoughtful ways that invite rich conversations. In popular culture, however, the relativism card is often played as a conversation stopper: your truth is yours and mine is mine and that's the end of the story.

In fact, there are genuine insights behind the

relativist impulse and none ends up threatening the idea that truth stands independently of what you or I happen to think about it. Let's return to the issue of how many words the Inuit have for snow. There may not be one definitive answer because there is more than one way of counting words. Inuit is a polysynthetic language in which multiple prefixes and suffixes can be attached to words in almost infinite ways, meaning that what counts as a word and what counts as a variant of a word is not always clear. Inuit is also not a single tongue but a family of closely related languages, so again there are questions about whether some small variations result in a different word or versions of the same one. We therefore have a number of different conventions we could choose to count the number of words, each one yielding a different number. But crucially, once we choose a convention to follow and count accordingly, our answer is determined by the facts, not us. I can choose how to count but the words out there to be counted exist whether I like it or not. Whether what we say is true or not depends on the world as well as our analytic framework. Not just any 'truth' is acceptable.

So although there is more than one truth to be told here, they do not contradict each other. Let's say one language distinguishes ten kinds of snow, another three and another just one. None of these languages need be wrong. All can be describing the same world, perfectly consistently. In the same way, to say it is good snow for skiing and bad snow for building an igloo is not to offer two competing truths about how good the snow is. The differences in our vocabularies concern which aspects of the world the different languages attend to. One language might be more fine-grained than the other, but what it is picking out could be equally real for a speaker of a simpler language. An Inuit could draw my attention to differences in the snow that I was not aware of without using Inuit words and I would still see what was there.

Languages might also be sensitive to different *contextual* features. When Westerners think of 'kinds of snow' they tend to think about how *the snow itself* is different. But it is perfectly possible that a language might distinguish between morning and evening snow, for example, not because the snow itself looks different under a microscope but because there are other reasons why it is important to know when the snow fell.

So there is more than one way of describing the world, more than one way of assigning value and importance to things. That does contradict a simplistic view that there is one and only one truthful way of talking. But who believes such a thing? There may be no one objective *truth* but there are objective *truths*, real truths about relative truths.

One reason so many seem reluctant to acknowledge this is that it would seem to make truth too clear-cut. True and false do not exhaust all the categories into which we can put statements. For instance, if you survey all Inuit speakers it might be indeterminate whether a particular word is distinct, a variant of another, or a piece of local slang. So it may be impossible to say how many words for snow there are.

We can and should grant that but all it shows, very helpfully, is that the defender of objective truth need not claim that all truths are clear and unequivocal. In this case, the truth would be that we can't say exactly how many words there are, but we can say something, objectively true: that there are around x words for snow, and the precise number is unclear for reasons that can be clearly explained. Objective truth does not always have sharp edges. Indeed, sometimes the truth precisely is that something is ambiguous or indeterminate, and the falsehood that something is clear-cut and determinate.

We should take Simon Blackburn's advice 'not to try to kill relativism, but to draw its teeth'.[33] We can do this by pointing out the mistake that is made when we confuse different perspectives on the truth with fundamental disagreements about what is actually true. To deny that a perspective captures the whole truth is not to deny that it captures some of it. That is why the phrase 'alternative facts' is so misguided. There are no *alternative* facts, just

75

additional facts we might have missed, or genuine facts that replace bogus ones.

The relativist impulse is by and large a noble one. It is opposed to the ownership of truth by one, usually privileged group; the crowding out of alternative perspectives; the simplification of complex reality. But none of this requires us to give up on truth. Indeed, it should require us to treasure it even more, because if none of these different ways of seeing and knowing is true in anything more than a personal or parochial way, why care about any of them? If what is true for me is not true for you then either one of us is wrong, or both of us have only one hand on the truth and need each other's help to see the whole of it. The panoply of legitimate perspectives should not therefore lead to the fragmentation of truth. Rather we should bring as many of these perspectives together as possible to create a fuller vision of reality.

8. Powerful truths

Fat is the major diet-based threat to human health. That, at least, was the mainstream view for several decades. However, it turns out that it is most probably false. While a diet very high in saturated or trans-fats is almost certainly bad for you, refined carbohydrates and especially sugars pose a greater risk to more people.

Too many point to *volte-faces* like this as evidence for the unreliability of science and medical expertise. As we have seen, evidence-based nutritional advice is bound to keep changing and evolving as we find out more. This is a sign that our understanding is developing as it should. What's more, such progress is more gentle than negative stereotypes about 'scientists always changing their minds' suggest. Between 1933 and 2014, for example, official advice in the UK on the optimal balance of calories from protein, fat and carbohydrate hardly shifted at all: 12 per cent from protein became 10–15 per cent, 27 per cent from fat increased slightly to 33 per cent, while 61 per cent from carbohydrates was cut a little to 50–55 per cent.[34] Details have changed, but the basic advice to eat proper foods, whole grains and plenty of fresh fruit and vegetables has been very consistent for decades. We should be not so much sceptical as tentative, recognising that nutritional science is relatively young and the last word on dietary advice has yet to be written.

However, all of this does not fully explain the change of heart over fat. The story is complicated by a factor that goes beyond evidence: power. In three separate ways, vested interests pushed the 'fat-is-bad' message in ways that distorted the scientific evidence.

Go back to the Second World War and sugar

was rightly being identified by the American Medical Association as having no contribution to make to a healthy diet. This suited the government of the day, which needed to ration it. Alarmed by this, the industry formed the Sugar Research Foundation (SRF), which despite its neutral, scientific sounding name existed solely to conduct and promote research that vindicated sugar. For instance, in 2016 it emerged that in the 1960s the SRF had paid three Harvard scientists to downplay the association between sugar consumption and heart disease and point the finger at saturated fat instead. All this promotion of the cause bore its plumpest fruit when the American Heart Association pinpointed fat and cholesterol as the prime causes of heart disease, a new orthodoxy known as the 'fat hypothesis', reflected in the US government's first dietary guidelines, published in 1980.

Arguably, however, the sugar industry's impact on the science was less significant than on the way it spun it. Food manufacturers tapped into the negative associations of fat to sell products as 'low fat' or 'fat-free' as though this made them healthier. Sometimes the health claims were overt: many 'healthy eating' ranges focused on low-fat foods. (One was even called 'lean cuisine'.) But very often no explicit health claim was made. It was enough to splash '95 per cent fat free' on the packaging and allow customers to draw their own, erroneous, conclusions. This was most cynical in low-fat cakes that contained even more sugar than their normal-fat equivalents.

However, as the writer Ian Leslie says, blame for the fat myth cannot entirely be 'laid at the door of corporate ogres'. Nutritional science got it wrong and a different kind of power helps explains why. It began in 1955 when the US President's chief physician announced that Eisenhower had suffered a heart attack. He went on to share the advice of a nutritionist called Ancel Keys to cut down on fat and cholesterol. Keys was the leading advocate of the fat hypothesis and with the aid of Eisenhower's endorsement, he gained more and more power in his field. 'He secured places for himself and his allies on the boards of the most influential bodies in American healthcare, including the American Heart Association and the National Institutes of Health,' Leslie says. 'From these strongholds, they directed funds to like-minded researchers, and issued authoritative advice to the nation.' While Keys was charismatic and forceful, his leading opponent, John Yudkin, was a 'mild-mannered man, unskilled in the art of political combat'.[35] In short, science took a wrong turn because the wrong scientist held too much power.

The story of fat is but one example of how what becomes accepted as true depends on more than facts or evidence. To control the 'truth' is to have great power, which is why anyone concerned with power and influence is also concerned to spin the truth in ways that suit them. Savvy citizens are right to be wary of anyone claiming to present the truth. We would always do well to ask, '*Cui bono?*' Who benefits from this version of 'truth'?

Michel Foucault is the philosopher most associated with the analysis of the relationship between truth and power. At times, his scepticism seemed to extend to claiming that what we call 'truth' is merely the expression of power. It is not difficult to see why this is the most common interpretation of his view. 'Truth isn't outside power, or lacking in power,' he argued. 'Truth isn't the reward of free spirits, the child of protracted solitude, nor the privilege of those who have succeeded in liberating themselves.'[36] He described the 'regimes of truth', the social mechanisms that determine who decrees something is true and on what basis. He concluded that '"Truth" is linked in a circular relation with systems of power which produce and sustain it, and to effects of power which it induces and which extend it.'

Whatever Foucault himself believed, we can agree that there is a great deal of power-play at work behind what gets accepted as true. But the force of his argument is severely diminished if we conclude that truth is *nothing more than* the exercise of power. For what would make that statement true? According to its own criteria, it would be nothing more than an attempt to take control of the notion of truth and put it in the hands of — what? French intellectuals? Foucault's argument is compelling only if we see it as truthfully describing the actual role of power of the world. In other words, to take it seriously we have to accept that there are at least some truths that are not merely expressions of power.

By adopting this attitude we are able to challenge the twisting of truth by power. We must be careful not to confuse the frequent capture of truth by power with an equation of truth and power. It was only because there were real truths about fat and sugar that people were able to expose the ways in which these facts had been hidden and twisted to suit the food industry. It is only because there are real truths about the effects of unregulated markets that an intellectual and moral case can be made against or for them that is not just a power struggle between people with different ideologies. It is only because truth is more than power that we can speak truth to power. Every time we debunk an alleged truth propounded by the self-interested powerful, we prove that truth can overcome power and must not always be its servant.

9. Moral truths

When it comes to many matters of fact, old-fashioned absolutism still usually trumps new-fangled relativism. People do not think the claim that Saddam Hussain had weapons of mass destruction is some people's legitimate truth. Many think it is unambiguously, completely false and those who claimed otherwise are liars who ought to be held to account for their deception. We don't sincerely doubt that facts are facts, no matter how much we doubt the authority or certainty of those who claim to have them.

When it comes to values, however, relativism has more genuine devotees. Partly this is a fruit of respect for diversity, often exacerbated by colonial guilt. All too aware of how arrogant oppressors condemned the practices of 'savage brutes' without any understanding, many are so eager to avoid repeating their errors that they feel it best to condemn nothing and leave each culture to itself. That's easy enough to do when the differences concern little more than customs or eating prohibitions. It's more difficult when those cultures practise things like female genital mutilation, male but not female polygamy, the persecution and even execution of homosexuals, the marriage of minors, the killing of *victims* of rape, or the control of the behaviour and dress of women much more than men. Few can go the whole way and accept that horrors like the Holocaust and child rape are only wrong for some. Despite all this, the Zeitgeist demands that we are as tolerant as possible, with 'Who are we to judge?' the default position.

Throwing up our hands is an understandable response if we believe that moral judgements involve facts about the rightness and wrongness of actions. Such moral facts are extremely elusive. Facts are established by appeal to evidence and observation. But what empirical discovery could demonstrate that murder is wrong? What experiment could we devise to test such a claim? Where under a microscope or through a telescope would we locate the moral essence of an action? We know that people *disapprove* of murder and that being killed is not good *for the victim*, but these facts do not prove that it is *wrong*. 'Wrong' is just the wrong kind of thing to be subjected to empirical demonstration.

But if we are not stating facts when we make moral claims, what are we doing? The obvious answer is simply expressing a preference, revealing our ethical tastes. But if that's right, then just as *de gustibus non est disputandum*, there's no disputing moral judgements either. Relativism seems to be the logical consequence of accepting there are no moral facts, and accepting this seems to be the rational consequence of empirically failing to find them.

There is, however, a middle way signposted

by David Hume's memorable line, 'reason is, and ought only to be, the slave of the passions'.[37] At first blush, this looks like classic relativism: our moral judgements merely reflect our feelings. But take away that 'merely' and something more interesting suggests itself. Morality for Hume is rooted not in rational argument or empirical demonstration but in fellow-feeling. What tells you murder is wrong is your ability to see things from the perspective of the victim, to see that to be deprived of life is to be deprived of something of supreme value. No logical proof is required for this. Indeed, if you cannot in a sense *feel* or *see* why life is of value, no logical argument could persuade you to *think* otherwise. The psychopath lacks not rationality but feeling.

Many are left deeply unsatisfied by this account of morality. If moral claims are not truth claims, then how do we arbitrate between them? Can we really be sanguine about the possibility that moral disagreement reduces to nothing more than differences in how we feel?

The unease can perhaps be ameliorated (if

not entirely removed) by seeing how truth is far from completely irrelevant to our moral deliberations. Hume himself unwittingly provides us with an example of this. A great moral philosopher he indisputably was, but that did not stop him affirming a common prejudice of his age. 'I am apt to suspect the Negroes, and in general all other species of men to be naturally inferior to the whites,' he wrote in a now infamous footnote.[38] That one of our greatest philosophers could write this is staggering and a salutary reminder that intelligence is no guarantee of virtue. It is vital to notice, however, that Hume's racism was not just an expression of a value or a feeling. It involved a factual mistake about the abilities and capacities of human beings. One of the most important reasons why attitudes to racism have changed is because claims of racial superiority and inferiority have come to be seen as factually incorrect.

Hume was right that, ultimately, morality is rooted in what he called 'moral sympathy'. But he did not stress enough the extent to which our feelings are shaped by what we take to be true, and so correcting false perceptions alters our moral judgements. When the facts change, we should not only change our minds but often our hearts. This is how moral progress has often proceeded. Greater concern for animal welfare followed on from an increasing belief that the idea that non-humans could not suffer was scientifically unsustainable. Belief that homosexuality is wrong has been undermined largely because people understand that sexual orientation is not (usually, at least) a choice and homosexuality is never an illness. Emitting pollutants and greenhouse gases has come to be seen as wrong entirely and only because the evidence shows it has harmful effects.

The idea that it is enlightened and progressive to refuse to insist that some moral values are better than others is therefore wrong-headed and pernicious. It is not simply a matter of different 'values', 'preferences' or even 'tastes'. Our moral views are intimately connected with how we see the world and a skewed perception can lead to a skewed morality, false beliefs to bad ethics. If we see the world truthfully we might not end up with complete moral agreement. We might agree, for instance, on how much inequality a certain political programme will create, and disagree about whether it is a price to pay for freedom, stability or some other good. But facts still matter, even in such cases, since it is only if we get them right that we can even see which moral judgement is preferable. If someone favours inequality in part because they believe it leads to greater wealth even for the poorest, it is important to know if such 'trickle down' economics actually works.

Often, truth plays an even more direct and important role. It is of more than etymological interest that 'prejudice' literally means pre-judgement (Latin: *prae* + *judicium*). Prejudice arises because we reach a conclusion *in advance* of seeing the relevant facts. When we judge *after* having seen the truth, prejudice is replaced by fair judgement. That's why although we may be wrong to talk about 'moral truths', truth has

91

a vital role in morality. Our moral judgements only carry weight when they accord with the facts both of human nature and the world. 'True theories are extremely valuable for the conduct of our lives as well as for the acquisition of knowledge,' wrote Aristotle, 'since because of their agreement with the facts they carry conviction, and so encourage those who understand them to live under their direction.'[39] Not anything goes, not least the idea that anything goes.

10. Holistic truths

Henry M. Morris lived into the twenty-first century but still believed that the earth was created by God less than 10,000 years ago. His 'young earth creationism' is widely dismissed as pseudoscience, but people like Morris are not stupid. In fact, they are often extremely clever and ingenious.

How else could they resist the apparently irrefutable scientific case that life has evolved on Earth over billions of years? Fossils are buried in the ground in layers that have clearly accumulated over time by processes geologists well understand. A range of scientific methodologies such as radiometric dating all point to the Earth being around four and half billion years old. Examination of DNA enables us to see how species are related to each other, and in particular how closely humans are in evolutionary terms to chimpanzees.

Young Earth Creationists can explain away all of this and more. Buried fossils are the result of the Great Flood which wiped out millions of animals, as described with historical accuracy in the Book of Genesis. Radiometric dating methods that suggest fossils and the Earth itself are older than this assume that everything in the world has always aged at a constant rate, but it is more than possible that nuclear decay rates, for example, were accelerated a billionfold or more during Creation week and the Flood. And the fact that chimpanzees and humans have a lot of shared DNA could just as easily point to a common designer as a common ancestor: Skodas are not descendants of the Volkswagens they resemble, they are simply made by the same company.

If all this is nonsense then it has to be

94

admitted it is all perfectly consistent nonsense. Indeed, if you believe in an omnipotent God, no evidence uncovered by mere mortals could prove anything about the ultimate nature or cause of the universe. Take evidence of the Earth's age. According to Genesis, when God created Adam and Eve, he created them as adults. That means that if you were to have examined them a week after their creation they would have had all the appearance of people who had been alive for around twenty years or more. The mere conceivability of their existence shows that something could theoretically be created with the appearance of age. In the same way, God could very easily have created the Earth with the appearance of a very long history. Fossils and even lights from distant stars could all be explained in this way. Maybe God created a pre-aged universe to see if we would choose our own best science over his revelation, as a test of our faith.

The search for a killer inconsistency in the Young Earth Creationist story is a doomed one.

Many objections can be met with impressive inventiveness. You don't think, for example, that Adam could possibly have named all the animals that walked the earth? Assume he only had to name all the genera, such as 'cat' and 'dog' rather than every species, so that if he named five a minute it would only have taken him around four hours.[40] But even when there is no explanation we can come up with, why should we expect mere humans to understand everything about God's creation? It's the logical version of heads I win, tails you lose. If I can rationally explain it, your objection is defeated; if I can't, it can be left as a divine mystery. No argument can defeat someone who thinks like this but, crucially, such a person is not being inconsistent.

Although the Byzantine ways in which such arguments are offered strikes most people as incredible, we all make use of the same basic holistic nature of justification. Truths do not stand or fall independently but are held in a network with other truths, all of which mutually support each other. Belief in the scientific evidence for evolution, for example, depends on belief in the general uniformity of nature over time and space; the ability of human beings to be able to see reality accurately and to understand it properly; the integrity of academic science and scientists. We arrive at truth holistically.

In our network of beliefs, however, not everything has the same importance. Some truths we take to be more fundamental than others. The naturalistic world view that gives rise to the big bang and evolution gives primacy to empirical evidence and our ability to understand it. This seems unproblematic to many but it has to be remembered that many serious philosophers have doubted that our sense experience, through which all empirical evidence is ultimately gained, gives us an accurate view of a mind-independent reality. None of the counter-arguments decisively defeats this scepticism. At best they are based on plausibility or probability, concluding that the view of the world as we perceive it as a kind of illusion is more outlandish than the idea that it has an objective existence with features we can at least in part discern. But the simplest explanation is not always the right one and 'plausibility' is not a precise concept. So not even our most fundamental tenets, the ones which hold the whole web of belief together, can be established with sufficient certainty that they demand universal assent.

Young Earth Creationists have different bedrocks, most importantly a belief that the Bible is the unerring word of God. Their reasons for believing this vary, but for many they are connected with a very strong experience of what they take to be a personal encounter with the divine, one which confirms their faith in the God of the Bible. To those who have not had such experiences, this seems a flimsy basis for such important beliefs. After all, haven't people all throughout history claimed to have had communion with God, experiences that contradict one another and therefore don't seem to be very reliable? True, but this is a probabilistic argument, not a conclusive one. If your sense of the divine is as strong to you as the feeling of gravity, isn't it in one sense as reasonable — at the very least understandable — to believe in one as the other? We all have to make some basic assumptions that we cannot afford to doubt. Belief in our very sanity is in some sense a leap of faith.

Because truths stand or fall together, it is not possible to put ourselves outside two webs of belief and assess their credibility from a third, neutral perspective. When naturalists conclude that the Young Earth Creationist world-view is not tenable, they do so from a naturalist perspective, and vice-versa. That is why it is so difficult to get to the 'bottom line' of truth. There is no such bottom line, only key threads that hold our beliefs together. This should teach us patience when it comes to trying to persuade others, as well as the realisation that sometimes we just won't be able to. When someone is really committed to keeping their familiar web intact, if anyone tries to break any of its links they will scurry around trying to patch it up at all costs, unaware that their fragile edifice is actually hanging by the slenderest of threads.

If beliefs form webs, then the metaphor suggests the worrying possibility that we might all be trapped in the version of the truth we have spun for ourselves. In one sense, this is obviously and sadly true. Changing minds is hard, precisely because changing our view of one important thing often requires us to challenge a whole load of other cherished opinions too. When someone decides Jesus is not the saviour after all, or that free trade is not the answer to all the world's economic ills, they do not just give up one belief but a whole way of seeing the world, a set of values, even often a network of friends. Beliefs are threads that if picked at can unravel the entire fabric they help keep together. Challenge someone's truth and often you challenge their whole world.

But that doesn't make us incapable of rigorous self-examination. We can turn and look honestly at our own webs, searching for what is well anchored and what lacks support, what forms a tight net and what leaves gaping holes. In that way we can make piecemeal corrections to our understanding of the world. We should not be too pessimistic, nor get so trapped by the web metaphor that we imagine our networks of belief to be less adaptable than they really are. Max Planck famously said that new scientific ideas take hold only when those who hold the old ones die off. In one sense this supports pessimism about the possibility of progress, but also that the truth will out in the end. His quip was also hyperbolic. If we are open and willing to change our minds, it is not inevitable that we will go to our graves denying the better picture of truth the new generation has painted.

There is similar hope in Thomas Kuhn's theory of scientific revolutions which, however imperfect, accurately identified the way in which a broad picture of reality exerts a grip on an intellectual community and shapes its thinking. Ultimately however, worse paradigms give way to better ones. Each revolution in thought brings the truth further out, even if none exposes it completely.

Science is a good example of a network of beliefs because it shows how truth-seeking is a collective enterprise. One weakness of the web metaphor is that it conjures an image of the solitary spider, weaving alone. In reality, each of our individual networks of belief is itself part of a wider, social network akin to the collaborative World Wide Web. We rely on the knowledge of others to construct our own best understanding of the truth.

The post-truth society is in part a result of a malfunctioning of this social system of knowledge. By retreating into bubbles of the like-minded, people can strip out a lot of inconvenient complexities a wider perspective would give, leading to a simpler but therefore also distorted network of belief. Falsehood masquerades as truth by retreating into incomplete networks of belief where convenient facts are overstated and inconvenient ones ignored or just simply denied.

No facts are inconvenient for the truth. The

way to truth is not to look for an impossible neutral view that takes us outside any given network of beliefs. It is to expand the web as much as we can, weaving in as many true threads as possible. Young Earth Creationists are very good at making their view consistent with the facts but the larger the network of facts they are forced to link up with, the more strained the connections become. When our coherent network of beliefs grows larger and is built on facts, each truth in it becomes stronger while every falsehood finds it harder to keep its place.

Conclusion: Future truths

If we desire to know the truth, it might be assumed that what we most need is a method of enquiry or a set of rules for establishing facts. The history of ideas is not short of such principles and procedures, be it the deductive reasoning of Descartes, the scientific method of Bacon, the study of revealed scriptures or the attainment of insight by disciplines of meditation and concentration. Our history suggests that more important than any of these is something more like an *attitude*. Establishing the truth requires 'epistemic virtues' like modesty, scepticism, openness to other perspectives, a spirit of collective enquiry, a readiness to confront power, a desire to create better truths, a willingness to let our morals be guided by the facts.

These epistemic virtues have become less evident in the post-truth world, as their corresponding vices have all become more common: overconfidence, cynicism, closed-mindedness, excessive individualism, passivity before power, loss of belief in the possibility of creating better truths, morals driven by a gut divorced from the head. Our greatest consolation in the post-truth world is that despite this, the epistemic virtues have not been widely, explicitly rejected nor the vices openly embraced. Most of us still value what the late Bernard Williams identified as the two key virtues of truth: sincerity and accuracy. These two virtues suggest the way in which truth requires the right relationship between the truth-seeker and the world: to get our facts right we need to get our attitudes to the facts right.

Truth is there if we are prepared to look for it even though it is far from plain or simple. We tend to think of truths as like shiny pebbles:

hard, unchangeable, clearly defined, collected in the mind as though it were a kind of rock garden. Truth is actually more like a real garden, an organic, holistic system where everything relates to everything else. While some features are as good as permanent, others grow, change or die. And like a garden, truth needs nurturing or else it becomes overgrown with the weeds of myth, distortions, misunderstandings and lies.

Truth is complicated but from each of the ten types of truth we have surveyed, a relatively simple rubric can be drawn to help us to make it flower:

- Spiritual 'truths' should not compete with secular ones but should seen as belonging to a different species.
- We should think for ourselves, not by ourselves.
- We should be sceptical not cynical.
- Reason demands modesty not certainty.
- To become smarter, we must understand the ways we are dumb.

- Truths need to be created as well as found.
- Alternative perspectives should be sought not as alternative truths but as enrichers of truth.
- Power doesn't speak the truth; truth must speak to power.
- For a better morality we need better knowledge.
- Truth needs to be understood holistically.

The defence of truth often takes the form of battles to defend particular truths that divide us. This is sometimes necessary but as the military metaphor suggests, it feeds antagonism. The greater, unifying enterprise is to defend the shared value we place on truth, the virtues that lead us towards it, and the principles that help us to identify it. Those who stand up for this are pushing at an open door because ultimately we all recognise that truth is not a philosophical abstraction. Rather it is central to how we live and make sense of ourselves, the world and each other, day by day.

Notes

1 Francis Bacon, *Novum Organum* (1620), Aphorism 9.

2 Alfred Tarski, 'Prace Towarzystwa Naukowego Warszawskiego' (The concept of truth in the languages of the deductive sciences) (1933), in *Wydzial III Nauk Matematyczno-Fizycznych 34*, reprinted in English in A. Tarski, *Logic, Semantics, Metamathematics, papers from 1923 to 1938*, ed. John Corcoran (Hackett Publishing Company, 1983).

3 Aristotle, *Metaphysics*, 1011b.

4 James Rothwell, 'Leading French philosopher: Marine Le Pen may win election as people have lost interest in whether politicians tell the truth', *Telegraph*, 20 November 2016.

5 Immanuel Kant, 'Answering the Question: What is Enlightenment?' (1784).

6 Plato, *Republic*, Book 2 (359a–360d).

7 'Political amateurs are conquering the world', Euronews, 14 November 2016, www.euronews.com/2016/11/14/
political-amateurs-are-conquering-the-world-beppe-grillo-tells-euronews

8 David Hume, *An Enquiry Concerning Human Understanding* (1748), Section 10.

9 J. B. Kennedy. *The Musical Structure of Plato's Dialogues* (Acumen, 2011).

10 Thomas Jefferson, Letter to Judge John Tyler Washington, 28 June 1804. www.let.rug.nl/
usa/presidents/thomas-jefferson/letters-of-thomas-jefferson/jefl164.php

11 René Descartes, *The Discourse on Method* (1637), Part 2, §19.

12 Spinoza, *Ethics* (1677), Part 1, Proposition VIII.

13 Spinoza, *Ethics* (1677), Part V, Proposition XXIII, Scholium.

14 Werner Heisenberg, *Physics and Philosophy* (1958), Chapter 5.

15 Hugo Mercier and Dan Sperber, *The Enigma of Reason* (Allen Lane, 2017), pp. 166, 171.

16 I offer a much more complete account of rationality in *The Edge of Reason* (Yale University Press, 2016).

17 Descartes used this phrase on several occasions.

18 The seminal collation of this research is Daniel Kahneman, *Thinking Fast and Slow* (Penguin, 2011).

19 Francis Bacon, *Novum Organum* (1620), Aphorism 70.

20 It first appeared in a late seventeenth-century volume called *Brief Lives* and is based on an account given to the author, John Aubrey, by the philosopher Thomas Hobbes.

21 R. Eccles, 'Acute cooling of the body surface and the common cold', *Rhinology* 40, pp. 109–114 (2002). www.rhinologyjournal.com/Rhinology_issues/109_Eccles

22 Ellen F. Foxman et al., 'Temperature-dependent innate defense against the common cold virus limits viral replication at warm temperature in mouse airway cells', *Proceedings of the National*

Academy of Sciences of the United States of America, vol. 112 no. 3, pp. 827–832, doi: 10.1073/pnas.1411030112. Reported at http://news.yale.edu/2015/01/05/

cold-virus-replicates-better-cooler-temperatures

23 David Hume, *An Enquiry Concerning Human Understanding* (1748), Section 4.

24 Aristotle, *Ethics*, 1146b.

25 Francis Bacon, *Novum Organum* (1620), Aphorism 97.

26 Quoted in Jonathan Israel, *A Revolution of the Mind* (Princeton University Press, 2010), p. 36.

27 J. L. Austin, *How to Do Things With Words* (Oxford University Press, 1962), p. 91.

28 Ron Suskind, 'Faith, Certainty and the Presidency of George W. Bush', *New York Times Magazine*, 17 October 2004. Rove was outed as the unnamed aide in this article by Mark Danner in 'Words in a Time of War: On Rhetoric, Truth and Power', in *What Orwell Didn't Know: Propaganda and the New Face of American Politics*, ed. András Szántó (PublicAffairs, 2007), p. 17.

29 Bush really did say this. On 6 November 2000,

the eve of the election, in his final stump speech he said of his opponents 'They misunderestimated me.'

30 Jane Mayer, 'Donald Trump's ghostwriter tells all', *New Yorker*, 25 July 2016.

31 Franz Boas, *Handbook of American Indian Languages* (Government Printing Office, 1911).

32 Roger Scruton, 'Some More -isms', in *Modern Philosophy* (1995), p. 32.

33 Simon Blackburn, 'After relativism', *Prospect*, 9 May 2013.

34 'Report of Committee on Nutrition', British Medical Association, Supplement to the *British Medical Journal*, 25 November 1933; Guideline Daily Amounts website hosted by the Food and Drink Federation, using official UK government figures, www.gdalabel.org.uk

35 Ian Leslie, 'The sugar conspiracy', *Guardian*, 7 April 2016.

36 'Truth and Power', an interview with Michel Foucault by Alessandro Fontana and Pasquale Pasquino in Michel Foucault, *Power/Knowledge: Selected Interviews and Other Writings*

1972–1977, ed. Colin Gordon (Pantheon Books, 1990).

37 David Hume, *A Treatise of Human Nature* (1739–40), Book 2, Part 3, §3.

38 David Hume, 'Of National Characters' (1753).

39 Aristotle, *Ethics*, 1172b.

40 https://answersingenesis.org/bible-characters/adam-and-eve/

Acknowledgments

My thanks, purely in alphabetical order, to the people who in various ways made this book possible and as good and truthful as it could be: John English, Lizzy Kremer, Bella Lacey, Antonia Macaro and Richard Milner.